Ten Poer
from Russ~~ia~~

C000091093

ex libris

Candlestick Press

Published by:
Candlestick Press,
Diversity House, 72 Nottingham Road, Arnold, Nottingham UK NG5 6LF
www.candlestickpress.co.uk

Design and typesetting by Diversity Creative Marketing Solutions Ltd.,
www.diversity.agency

Printed by Ratcliff & Roper Print Group, Nottinghamshire, UK

Selection and Introduction © Boris Dralyuk, 2018

Cover illustration © Irina Kildiushova/Shutterstock

Candlestick Press monogram © Barbara Shaw, 2008

© Candlestick Press, 2018
in association with Pushkin Press

ISBN 978 1 907598 70 8

Acknowledgements:

The poems in this pamphlet are reprinted from the following books,
all by permission of the publishers listed unless stated otherwise.
Every effort has been made to trace the copyright holders of the poems
published in this book. The editor and publisher apologise if any material
has been included without permission or without the appropriate
acknowledgement, and would be glad to be told of anyone who has not
been consulted. Thanks are due to all the copyright holders cited below
for their kind permission:

Anna Akhmatova (1889-1966), 'In Memory of Sergey Yesenin', trans. by
Boris Dralyuk, *The Penguin Book of Russian Poetry*, edited by Robert
Chandler, Irina Mashinski and Boris Dralyuk (Penguin Classics, 2015),
by kind permission of the translator and the FTM Agency.

Nikolay Gumilyov (1886-1921), 'The Lost Tram', trans. by Boris
Dralyuk, *The Penguin Book of Russian Poetry*, edited by Robert
Chandler, Irina Mashinski and Boris Dralyuk (Penguin Classics, 2015),
by kind permission of the translator.

Georgy Ivanov (1894-1958), 'I still find charm', trans. by Boris Dralyuk,
The Penguin Book of Russian Poetry, edited by Robert Chandler,
Irina Mashinski and Boris Dralyuk (Penguin Classics, 2015), by kind
permission of the translator.

Yuri Kazarnovsky (1905-1960), 'The Stroll', trans. by Boris Dralyuk, first published in this anthology.

Mikhail Lermontov (1814-1841), 'My Country', trans. by Peter France, *The Penguin Book of Russian Poetry* (Penguin Classics, 2015), by kind permission of the translator.

Osip Mandelstam (1891-1938), 'Take from my palms', trans. by Peter France, *Poems of Osip Mandelstam* (New Directions Poetry Pamphlet, 2014), by kind permission of the translator.

Julia Nemirovskaya (b. 1962), 'Bouquet', trans. by Boris Dralyuk, first appeared in Russian in *PLAVUCHII MOST: Russian and World Poetry Magazine*, 2016 #1 (9), will be published in *Tretia knizhechka* (Moscow: Vodolei, 2019), by kind permissions of the author and translator.

Boris Pasternak (1890-1960), 'Hamlet', trans. by Robert Chandler, *The Penguin Book of Russian Poetry*, edited by Robert Chandler, Irina Mashinski and Boris Dralyuk (Penguin Classics, 2015), by kind permission of the translator and the FTM Agency.

Alexander Pushkin (1799-1837), Prologue to 'Ruslan and Lyudmila', trans. by Peter France, *The Penguin Book of Russian Poetry*, edited by Robert Chandler, Irina Mashinski and Boris Dralyuk (Penguin Classics, 2015), by kind permission of the translator.

Marina Tsvetaeva (1892-1941), 'To Alya', trans. by Boris Dralyuk, first published in this anthology.

All permissions cleared courtesy of Swift Permissions (swiftpermissions@gmail.com).

Where poets are no longer living, their dates are given.

Contents

Introduction

Those who study Russian literature soon learn that, "In Russia, a poet is more than a poet". The fact that this oracular adage, known to virtually all Russians, is itself a line of poetry – written by Yevgeny Yevtushenko (1932 – 2017), whose readings attracted stadium-size crowds in the 1960s – testifies to its accuracy. Few cultures attach so much significance to verse, for better or worse. Indeed, historically, Russian poets have borne a mammoth, all too often a crushing burden. They have been looked to – variously or all at once – as carriers of the national idea, voices of dissent, embodiments of personal freedom, and prophets of the coming day.

This tradition – and modern Russian literature as we know it – began with Alexander Pushkin (1799 – 1837), whose prologue to *Ruslan and Lyudmila* (1820), his first major poem, opens this selection. Drawing on disparate elements of Slavic lore, Pushkin weaves together a variegated romantic tapestry that has, for two centuries, served as a primer on Russian culture, more effective than any textbook. Like most Russian speakers, I learned Pushkin's lines by heart as a child, and imagined the scenes they depict each night as I drifted off to sleep. Pushkin's great successor, Mikhail Lermontov (1814 – 1841), the Byron of Russian verse, presents a more complicated attitude towards his native land in 'My Country'. Here we see the peculiar charm of the Russian landscape – its wide rivers, deep forests, bright meadows, and white birches, but also its coldness, squalor, and drunkenness. To love this country is to love it "with a strange love – / stronger than reason!"

That kind of irrational passion, which swings wildly from adoration to hatred, is one of the main currents of Russian culture. Its traces are evident not only in Russian poetry but also in the lives of its creators. Both Pushkin and Lermontov were killed in duels; other poets issued conscientious but self-destructive challenges to a murderous state; and others yet took their own lives. Boris Pasternak (1890 – 1960) dramatizes the fate of the Russian poet in his late masterpiece 'Hamlet', which was included in *Doctor Zhivago*, and Anna Akhmatova (1889 – 1966) reflects on it in her piercing, characteristically crystalline lyric dedicated to Sergey Yesenin, who hanged himself in 1925 at the age of 30. Her words apply just as readily to her former husband Nikolay Gumilyov (1886 – 1921), who was executed by the Bolshevik regime, to her friend Osip Mandelstam (1891 – 1938), who perished in the Gulag, and to Vladimir Mayakovsky (1893 – 1930) and Marina Tsvetaeva (1892 – 1941), who committed suicide.

These tragic stories shouldn't lead one to believe that Russian poetry is a joyless affair. On the contrary, the same poets who lived forever within reach of the "shaggy paw / of voiceless terror" appeared to have special access to the sublime. Tsvetaeva's exuberant poem addressed to her daughter Ariadna, whom she called Alya, is a perfect expression of the Russian notion of freedom – heedless and unbounded – while Mandelstam's mellifluous 'Take from my palms…' is as sweet as any fruit of Hellas, to which he was so devoted. There is even a certain agonized, delirious joy in Gumilyov's 'The Lost Tram', one of his last poems. This proto-surrealist nightmare vision of pre-Revolutionary Russia falling at the feet of a monstrous executioner was written exactly a century after Pushkin's fairy tale prologue. One marks the beginning of modern Russian literature; the other marks the end of its pre-Soviet period.

Any anthology, no matter how expansive, is necessarily reductive. At its best, it is an entryway – a corridor full of inviting doors, which open onto rooms that contain many wonders, as well as many other doors… My goal in compiling this brief selection was to indicate the depth and breadth of the Russian poetic tradition. I wanted to touch on its cornerstones, but also to illuminate a few of its hidden corners. To that end, I've included a poem by Yuri Kazarnovsky (1905 – 1960), who spent many years in the Gulag and happened to be among the last people to see Mandelstam alive. His witty, light-hearted 'The Stroll' bears few marks of the many hardships he had suffered throughout his life and instead playfully captures the minor indignity of an old man's hopeless infatuation with a young woman. The collection closes with two lyrics by Russian émigré poets. Georgy Ivanov's (1894 – 1958) 'I still find charm…' is an existentialist statement with an exquisite image at its heart, and Julia Nemirovskaya's (b. 1962) equally exquisite 'Bouquet', written more than half a century later, adds a striking spiritual dimension to Ivanov's fading flower. I welcome the reader to enter this small corridor. In Pushkin's words, "All Rus's magic lies in wait!"

Boris Dralyuk

Prologue to Ruslan and Lyudmila

On the curved strand a green oak grows,
on the green oak a golden chain,
and on it round and round there goes
the cat of knowledge, night and day –
goes to the right and sings a ditty,
goes to the left, begins a tale.

Strange beings are there: there roams the *leshy*, *
a mermaid swings a fishy tail;
there on the paths untrod by humans
are footprints of unheard-of beasts;
a house on chicken's legs from romance
stands without windows, doors or gates;
there hill and dale are full of visions;
there as dawn comes, the waves are breaking
upon an empty, sandy shore,
there Baba Yaga's fearful mortar
comes rushing home with clash and clatter;
there golden Kashchey meets his fate…
All Rus's magic lies in wait!
There too was I, and sipped the honey;
the green oak by the strand I saw;
beneath its shade the cat of knowledge
told me its tales. I can recall
just one of them, and over tea
I'll tell it to society.

Alexander Pushkin (1799 – 1837)
Translated by Peter France

* *leshy:* a forest spirit.

My Country

I love my country, but with a strange love –
stronger than reason! …
Neither the fame that blood can buy,
nor the calm pride of confidence,
nor the time-honoured gifts of ignorant days
can stir my soul with dreams of happiness.

But what I love – for some strange reason –
is the cold silence of her plains,
the swaying branches of her endless forests,
her rivers as wide-spreading as the sea;
galloping in a cart on country tracks
and gazing slowly deep into the dark,
seeing on either side, longing for sleep,
the poor sad villages' bright windows.
I love the smoke of burning stubble,
the lines of carts crossing the steppe,
and in bright meadows, on a hill,
a pair of birches gleaming white.
I feel a pleasure few can share
seeing the barns piled high with grain,
the hut beneath a roof of thatch
with fretted shutters on the windows;
and on a dewy feast-day evening
I'll gaze till late into the night
at whistling dancers, stamping feet,
and hear the drunken peasants talk.

Mikhail Lermontov (1814 – 1841)
Translated by Peter France

To Alya

And when you too are dragged – as by a tide –
into a life of endless wandering,
justify your snakish pedigree:
put home – myself – my poems – out of mind.

Know one thing: you will be old tomorrow.
Drink wine, ride troikas, sing loud in the bar-room,
be a blue-eyed gypsy, be a temptress.
Know one thing: you'll never find an equal –
so throw yourself at every lover's breast.

Oh, the blazing Paris boulevards!
(Do you see them? Millions of eyes!)
Oh, the thunder of Madrid's guitars!
(I've written of them – oh so many times!)

Know one thing: (your gaze is wide and ardent,
the sails are swelling – on your merry way!)
Know one thing: you will be old tomorrow –
child, nothing else is worth the time of day.

Marina Tsvetaeva (1892 – 1941)
Translated by Boris Dralyuk

"Take from my palms some sun…"

Take from my palms some sun to bring you joy
and take a little honey – so the bees
of cold Persephone commanded us.

No loosing of the boat that is not moored,
no hearing of the shadow shod in fur,
no overcoming fear in life's dense wood.

And kisses are all that's left us now,
kisses as hairy as the little bees
who perish if they fly out of the hive.

They rustle in transparent depths of night,
their home dense forests on Taigetos' slopes,
their food is honeysuckle, mint and time.

So for your joy receive my savage gift,
a dry and homely necklace of dead bees
who have transmuted honey into sun.

Osip Mandelstam (1891 – 1938)
Translated by Peter France

In Memory of Sergey Yesenin

There are such easy ways
to leave this life,
to burn to an end
without pain or thought,
but a Russian poet
has no such luck.
A bullet is more likely
to show his winged soul
the way to Heaven;
or else the shaggy paw
of voiceless terror will squeeze
the life out of his heart
as if it were a sponge.

Anna Akhmatova (1889 – 1966)
Translated by Robert Chandler

The Lost Tram

I was walking down an unfamiliar street,
and suddenly I heard the caws of crows,
and distant thunder, and a ringing lute:
a tram flew by before my eyes.

Just how I ran onto its running board
remains a mystery.
The tail it trailed, even in daylight,
was firebird-fiery.

It raced on like a dark and winged whirlwind,
adrift in time's abyss...
Stop, tram-driver,
stop this tram at once.

Too late. We've turned the corner,
glided through a palm-oasis,
and rocked our way across three bridges –
the Neva, the Nile, the Seine.

Slipping past the window, an ancient beggar
threw us a searching stare –
the beggar who died in Beirut, of course,
only last year.

Where am I? Languid, anxious,
my heart beats in response:
'Look – it's the station! They're selling tickets
to India of the Soul – depart at once!'

A sign... It announces in blood-swollen letters:
'Greengrocer.' I know that instead
of cabbage heads, swedes and rutabagas
they sell the heads of the dead.

The executioner, with a face like an udder,
red-shirted, stout as an ox,
has chopped off my head. Along with the others,
it lies at the bottom of a slippery box.

On a side street, a house of three windows,
a fence made of boards, greying grass...
Stop, tram-driver,
stop this tram at once.

Mashenka, you lived and sang here.
Here's where you wove me a carpet.
Where are they now – your voice, your body?
My dear, are you truly among the dead?

O how you moaned in your chamber,
while I, in a powdered wig, your groom,
went to present myself to the Empress –
never to glimpse you again.

I've grasped it at last: our freedom
is only a light pulsating from far –
people and shadows stand at the entrance
to the zoo of the wandering stars.

A sweet and familiar wind, of a sudden,
and over the bridge, flying my way –
a horseman's hand in a glove of iron,
and two great hooves, raised to the sky.

Steadfast stronghold of Orthodoxy,
St. Isaac's spire is etched on high.
Prayers must be sung for Mashenka's health
and a memorial service for me.

And still, my heart is forever sullen.
It's hard to breathe, and it hurts to live...
Mashenka, I could never have known
of such a love, of such a grief.

Nikolay Gumilyov (1886 – 1921)
Translated by Boris Dralyuk

Hamlet

The hum dies down; alone on stage,
my back against the wall, I try
to sense within a distant echo
the twists and turns of destiny.

A thousand glinting opera glasses
focus the dark into my eyes.
O Father, should it be possible –
allow this cup to pass me by.

I like your stubborn, bold design,
and I've agreed to play this part.
But other forces are at play now –
this once, please count me out...

The acts cannot be rearranged
and there's no turning from the road.
Alone, a sea of cant all round me:
life is not a walk across a field.

Boris Pasternak (1890 – 1960)
Translated by Robert Chandler

The Stroll

Yes, I remember… And the shadow
of someone else's grief descends:
a blindman met us in the morning –
but couldn't meet your lovely glance.

I gaze at you… And blindly trust
that muteness is more frightening yet:
a mute man who sat down beside us
could offer you no compliment.

A streak of smoke… Whine of a motor…
I marvel, can't believe it's true:
a pilot flies his jet – a hero…
He flies so fast… And not to you?

A car darts by, clashing with wind.
Its driver is as pale as chalk:
his is the pallor of deep pain –
because he couldn't whisk you off.

Chopin… And wreaths… And through your lashes
the sadness of huge eyes shines blue…
Oh, how I pity the poor soldier
who died for anyone but you.

Still, I'm unhappier than others –
the poet is a bit too old…
Where can I find you magic glasses
that would remove ten years or so?

Yuri Kazarnovsky (1905 – 1960)
Translated by Boris Dralyuk

"I still find charm…"

I still find charm in little accidental
trifles, empty little things –
say, in a novel without end or title,
or in this rose, now wilting in my hands.

I like its moiré petals, dappled
with trembling silver drops of rain –
and how I found it on the sidewalk,
and how I'll toss it in a garbage can.

Georgy Ivanov (1894 – 1958)
Translated by Boris Dralyuk

Bouquet

No, I won't throw it out, for the sake of that tulip:
still fresh and so white, that satiny curl –
a sea-captain's collar folded over his tunic,
a theatrical backcloth, like a windowless wall.
Its petals are like cupped and half-turned palms,
its bloom a head, a gleaming cherry in its mouth.

...If it must go, let somebody else throw it out –
as God will say of me when my turn comes.

Julia Nemirovskaya
Translated by Boris Dralyuk